Waffen-SS
1943 KURSK

5

ARCHIVE SERIES

Waffen-SS
1943 KURSK

Photo Editor
Remy Spezzano

RZM
PUBLISHING

Photo Editor: Remy Spezzano

First Published August 2004
by
RZM Imports, Inc.
One Pomperaug Office Park, Suite 102
Southbury, CT 06488 USA
Tel. 203-264-0774 Fax. 203-264-4967
e-mail: rzm@rzm.com
www.rzm.com
Text and Captions by George Nipe
Layout and Design by Todd Rose
Text edited by Jeffery Hufnagel
Jacket Design by Todd Rose

Photograph Credits:
U.S. National Archives

Printed and Bound in Spain
by
Zure

ISBN 0-9748389-0-X

n the first days of July 1943, six professional photo-journalists serving with the Waffen-SS Propaganda Company set out to capture on film Germany's first major military summer offensive, known today as the Battle of Kursk. Armed with the latest model 35mm Leica cameras, these men lived on the front lines, photographing what historians would later declare the largest tank battle in history.

Presented on the pages of this special six-volume series are those precious images. Each of the photographers was attached to one of the major Waffen-SS fighting divisions.

Their names and units are as follows:

Johan King	SSLAH
Max Büschel	SSLAH
Hugo Lindekens	SSLAH
Willi Merz	SSTK
Hermann Groenert	SSTK
Hans Cantzler	SSTK

Unfortunately, during the closing days of World War II an order was given by the Reichssichersheitshauptamt ("National Security Service Main Office") to destroy all photographs and negatives pertaining to the Waffen-SS contained in the office of the Propaganda Company headquarters in Berlin.

As fate would have it, a small collection of original 35mm contact sheets did manage to survive, 28 of which contained images from the Battle of Kursk. Thanks to recent advancements in digital technology we have been able to resurrect and preserve these rare images, once thought lost forever. Although much continues to be written on this battle, the images in this series represent the only German visual link we have to this major event for future generations.

With 500 individual frames to work from, much pain-staking care was taken in the preparation of this collection. This archival series presents the best images from each roll of film, displayed in the order they were taken by each photographer, with individual attention provided to each photograph's aesthetic presentation on the page. I have personally inspected and worked on each image contained within the pages of this series in order to ensure the best quality possible. In doing so, my personal respect for the work of these men, along with the courage of those captured in the photographs, has only grown.

It is my hope that this series provides a visual bridge between you and those who took part in this historical battle, while providing an excellent addition to your military reference library.

Remy Spezzano, Publisher
RZM Imports, Inc.
September, 2002

The Battle of Kursk took place in the southern Ukraine during the summer of 1943 and was the last major German offensive in Russia. Preparations for the operation, which was code named "Citadel," began in April 1943, after the conclusion of the strategically important Battle of Kharkov. The starting date of the operation was postponed several times by Hitler until he decided upon the night of July 4th-5th. The objective of "Citadel" was to eliminate a huge bulge that protruded fifty miles westward into the German lines. The plan was to cut off the bulge at its base by attacks from the north and south, thereby encircling and destroying the Soviet armies in the salient. After inflicting this defeat upon the Russians, Hitler hoped to be able to transfer first-class German divisions from Russia to France to oppose the expected invasion by the Western Allies.

The attack force in the south consisted of two armies of Field Marshal Erich von Manstein's Army Group South, the 4th Panzer Army, commanded by Colonel General Hermann Hoth, and Armee-abteilung Kempf, led by General of Panzer Troops Werner Kempf. The two armies were to launch parallel attacks north from the Belgorod area, drive to Kursk and link up with the German 9th Army that was attacking southward. The 4th Panzer Army consisted of the 48th Panzer Corps and the IInd SS Panzer Corps under command of SS-Obergruppen-führer Paul Hausser. The three divisions of the SS Panzer Corps were the 1st SS Panzer-Grenadier Division "Leibstandarte," the 2nd SS Panzer-Grenadier

Division "Das Reich" and the 3rd SS Panzer-Grenadier Division "Totenkopf." These divisions had to be rebuilt following the Kharkov fighting due to their enormous losses: 11,500 killed and wounded. Thousands of new recruits, many of whom were only 17 or 18 years old, arrived from Waffen-SS training and replacement units. The new soldiers received intensive classroom training, weapons instruction and took part in live-fire combat training exercises upon replicas of Russian fortifications.

While the Germans prepared for the summer offensive, the Russians fortified the entire Kursk salient. The Soviet Army conscripted more than 100,000 civilian workers to help dig trenches and construct bunkers and other fortifications. Tactically important hills were fortified with complex trench systems, dug-in tanks and camouflaged bunkers. Most of these hills were protected with a fifteen to twenty foot deep anti-tank ditch that was screened by a broad minefield. In addition, the Soviet Army amassed huge operational and strategic reserves consisting of numerous tank and infantry armies arrayed in the strategic depths of the Soviet defensive system.

On the night of July 4th-5th, preliminary assaults by "Leibstandarte" and "Das Reich" broke into the first belt of Soviet defenses. By the end of July 5th, the two divisions had reached the forward edge of the second belt while "Totenkopf" secured the Corps' eastern flank. At the end of July 6th, both "Leibstandarte" and "Das Reich" were through the second Soviet belt of fortifications, driving toward the town of Prochorowka, near the strategic Psel River bend. The SS divisions, particularly "Leibstandarte," advanced much quicker than either the 48th Panzer Corps or the 3rd Panzer Corps that were attacking to the left and right respectively. The 3rd Panzer Corps remained stuck west of Belgorod until the night of July 10th, while the 48th Panzer Corps lost most of its armor in the first two days, including nearly 75% of the 195 new Panther tanks attached to Panzer Grenadier Division "Grossdeutschland." During the following day, both Panzer corps struggled to close up on the flanks of Hausser's formations. As a result, the SS divisions were attacked continually by reserve Soviet tank corps on both flanks due to the failure of the army corps to keep pace with their SS comrades and provide defense. This critical failure prevented Hausser from attacking with all three of his divisions on line, critically reducing the power of the advance by IInd SS Panzer Corps.

On July 9th, "Leibstandarte" renewed its attacks toward Prochorowka while "Totenkopf" regrouped to thrust northward toward the Psel River. "Das Reich" was forced to take over much of the defense of the eastern flank, repelling attacks by the Soviet 2nd, 2nd Guards and 5th Guards Tank Corps south of Prochorowka. Heavy rains turned roads into nearly impassable tracks of deep, black mud that made supply extremely difficult and greatly delayed movement of combat units. Early morning fog and violent thunderstorms impeded visibility so drastically that Luftwaffe air support often could not be utilized. Yet, even with such poor weather conditions, the Russians seemed to find a way to get their planes into the air. In spite of the mud, supply problems and increasing Soviet air strength "Leibstandarte" battled slowly toward Prochorowka while "Das Reich" fought off heavy tank attacks from the east.

"Totenkopf" began its initial assault on the Psel River on July 10th with the Panzer-Grenadiers of Regiment "Totenkopf" assaulting the river defenses at dawn. Following bloody fighting the regiment established a foothold on the northern bank by the late afternoon. Meanwhile "Leibstandarte" and "Das Reich" fought off assaults by the 2nd, 2nd Guards, 5th Guards Tank Corps and 10th Tank Corps. On July 11th, "Leibstandarte" was two kilometers from the edge of Prochorowka and "Das Reich" had blunted the Soviet thrusts against the Corps' flank. In spite of deep mud, constantly interrupted supply and Soviet counterattacks two bridges were built across the river and "Totenkopf's" Panzer regiment crossed over into the bridgehead. Hausser intended to assault Prochorowka from three directions on July 12th. However, unknown to the Germans, the entire Soviet 5th Guards Tank Army under command of Lieutenant General P.A. Rotmistrov had arrived at Prochorowka on the night of July 11th.

With over 600 tanks of his own and reinforced by 250 tanks of the 2nd and 2nd Guards Tank Corps, Rotmistrov launched a ferocious attack upon the IInd SS Panzer Corps on the morning of July 12th.

German records show that Hausser's three divisions possessed slightly over two hundred tanks by that time, giving the Russians a numerical superiority in tanks of more than four to one. In spite of this advantage, the SS divisions blunted Rotmistrov's attacks, inflicting tank losses upon the Soviet formations of eight Russian tanks for every one SS tank lost. "Totenkopf's" Panzergruppe then drove northward from the river and reached a key road north of the bridgehead that was to be the German high-water mark in the south. However, after the heavy casualties and severe emotional strains of the battle of Prochorowka, the troops of the SS divisions were exhausted physically and mentally. The vicious fighting to penetrate fortified lines of defense while contending with unending flank attacks by waves of Soviet operational and strategic reserves had taken their toll. After July 12th, neither "Leibstandarte" nor "Totenkopf" were able to mount any significant offensive operations, although "Totenkopf" successfully turned back all attempts by the Soviet 1st Tank Army and the newly arrived 5th Guards Army to drive it out of the Psel bridgehead.

The 3rd Panzer Corps finally closed up on the SS right flank on July 15th, but that final lunge north came too late. Hitler had already canceled the offensive, although he allowed Manstein a few days to try to destroy the armored elements of the 5th Guards Tank Army. "Das Reich" made one last attempt to reach Prochorowka, however by July 15th the division's advance bogged down in mud and a stubborn Russian defense a few kilometers south of Prochorowka. On the following day Hausser ordered the Corps to regroup for other missions, marking the end of the offensive operations by the IInd SS Panzer Corps during Operation Citadel. "Totenkopf" held on to its bridgehead in spite of continuous Soviet attacks, not pulling back across the river until ordered to do so on the night of July 17th-18th. Shortly afterward Hitler decided to send "Leibstandarte" to Italy in order to rebuild it once again. Meanwhile, "Das Reich" and "Totenkopf" were sent south to the Armeeabteilung Hollidt sector to repulse a dangerous Soviet attack in the Mius River sector.

Without any fresh Panzer divisions to throw into the battle, Manstein had no hope of further success, and Operation Citadel came to a fitful end. With the failure of the operation, the initiative on the Eastern Front was irretrievably lost and Germany remained on the strategic defensive until the end of the war.

Panzers from "Das Reich" assemble on the open steppe southwest of Prochorowka.

The crews use this time to prepare their vehicles for the ensuing battle.

A "Das Reich" halftrack, towing an anti-tank gun, moves forward to the next engagement.

A column of halftracks, the first vehicle armed with a 2cm Flak gun, move down a dusty Ukrainian road.

The halftracks, some of which are painted in camouflage patterns, pass a civilian vehicle.

Stirring up clouds of dust, and thus inviting Soviet air attacks, the "Das Reich" halftracks continue to roll through a typical Ukrainian town.

Halftracks and trucks roll northwards towards new positions a few kilometers southwest of Prochorowka in order to protect the exposed right flank of "Leibstandarte".

A Panzer III bogged down in the mud, after its crew misjudged the off-road terrain.

A crewman inspects the muddied track and drive sprocket.

In a short moment, Panzer 514 will be pulled back onto the road by another tank.

A foliage covered Panzer IV on the move, its camouflage paint scheme clearly visible on the side skirts.

Soviet T–34 tanks in German service, almost surely belonging to "Das Reich".

A motorcycle sidecar team takes a short pause for a refreshing drink.

An SS man shares a smoke with an army enlisted man in care of a pair of horses.

"Das Reich" supply and transport vehicles keep the division on the move.

The devastation of war!
Two Ukrainian women and a
child sit despondently in the
ruins of their village.

A young calf has been
commandeered.

"Leibstandarte" Tiger number 1313, commanded by SS-Unterscharführer Otto Augst. Standing in the cupola is the gunner, SS-Sturmann Heinrich Knöss.

An unfortunate Ukrainian woman with child tearfully describes her situation to the kneeling SS soldier as the smoke of her ravaged home rises behind them.

Several SS men inspect a Soviet Yak-1 fighter plane shot down by Flak gunners.

An ammunition belt of 12.7mm shells, deadly effective in attacks upon personnel and soft-skinned military vehicles.

The Russian nickname for the Yak-1 was "Ubiytsa" ("killer"). Because of its silhouette, the Germans labeled it the "Russian Spitfire".

A message written on the fighter's tail warns against scavenging the plane's guns or parts.

SS-Grenadiers take shelter in a trench knowing that the next day would bring heavy fighting.

A battery of 15cm howitzers prepares to fire in support of the attack.

A gunner checks the firing coordinates while another member of the crew takes time to grab a quick bite of food.

"Feuer!" The howitzer roars, sending its shell towards its target while the crew plugs their ears to avoid damage to their hearing.

Another SS man nonchalantly eats from his mess kit while in the background the heavy guns continue to fire.

The gun in full recoil. In the foreground a crewman screws a fuse into the nose of the next shell to be fired.

shell casing is removed
n the breech of the gun.

More ammunition is brought forward in their protective wicker containers.

The shell and powder have been placed in the breech. The lanyard is pulled and another round is on the way.

A captured T–34 is put into service
by "Das Reich".

Another T-34 pressed into German service.

A section leader provides first aid to a wounded comrade of his unit.

Finding safe shelter in a captured anti-tank ditch, one man stays awake, while another slumps over in exhaustion.

A "Leibstandarte" motorcycle team; the men on the right have fallen asleep, one with a cigarette hanging from his lips, while the man in the foreground industriously cleans his rifle.

SS–Grenadiers
resting in a shallow
Soviet tank ditch.

Soviet prisoners of war march to the rear after being captured. The various racial groups under Soviet rule are quite obvious in this photo.

A British Churchill tank, heavily armored but poorly gunned and not favored by the Russian tank crews.

An SS reconnaissance unit scouts out Soviet positions.

The vast array of vehicles in this unit is quite impressive.

A forward observer scans the horizon for enemy troop positions.

"Das Reich" battalion commander SS-Sturmbannführer Vincenz Kaiser stands in his command vehicle.

SS-Grenadiers enter a recently cleared village, accompanied by captured Soviet soldiers.

The village has been cleared and both SS soldiers and prisoners move forward with caution.

Smoke from the burning village creates an eerie fog.

Carrying a steel ammo box this SS man grins for the camera while passing a Russian soldier who clearly does not have as much to smile about.

The commander of a halftrack company studies his map while standing in his foliage draped command vehicle.

"Das Reich's" captured T-34s engage in the battle!

Tank battle! Artillery rounds explode ahead of this regimental command tank.

A lone Tiger rolls over the empty, featureless steppe, its gun turned to the right as the commander peers out of the open cupola.

During a break in the fighting the gunner of Tiger number S13 takes on extra 88 shells, handing them through the rear turret escape hatch to another member of the crew.

The fighting over for now, a "Das Reich" Tiger number S21 rolls toward the sound of the guns with its commander searching the horizon for the next target.

A halftrack rolls into battle with a half squad of Grenadiers ready to leap out and attack.

Standing near a well-camouflaged halftrack, two "Leibstandarte" small unit commanders study the approaches to a Russian position, searching for the best route of attack.

Peiper's battalion on the attack!

The vehicle on the left is a "Grille", armed with a 15cm infantry howitzer.

A motorcycle and sidecar combination moves through the high grass during a lull in the fighting.

This motorcycle crew takes a few moments to relax while in the rear
another Grenadier stands on the front of a halftrack, peering into
the distance.

SS-Untersturmführer Werner Wolff, adjutant of III./ SS-Pz.Gren.Rgt. 2
(the halftrack battalion commanded by Joachim Peiper).

A knocked out British Churchill tank, one of hundreds of Churchills, Cromwells, and Valentine tanks provided to the Russian Army as part of the Lend Lease program.

The tank has obviously suffered considerable damage to its side and hull, due to German heavy artillery.

A short distance behind the lines a Panzergrenadier unit attends to everyday tasks.

The men line up at a captured well to fill their mess kits and buckets.

An SS–Panzer crewman operates the well, certainly providing the most appreciated work of the day.

PHOTO CAPTIONS

Page 10: On July 11th, "Das Reich" began to turn over major sections of its front to the 167th Infantry Division. The three regiments of the division occupied the positions formerly held by the SS Grenadiers, allowing "Das Reich" to assemble closer to Prochorowka. **KB: Merz 14**

Page 11: Note the Kursk divisional marking on the front hull. The Panzer IVs and IIIs were provided with additional armor plating to protect running gear and turrets. Wheels and sections of track were stored so as to function as improvised armor. **KB: Merz 14**

Page 12: On July 11th, after spending two days in reserve at Oserowskij repairing its battle damaged tanks, the division's Panzer battalion had 34 Panzer IIIs, 18 Panzer IVs, 8 T-34s and one Tiger tank. Including seven Befehlpanzers, the division possessed a total of 68 operational tanks on that date. **KB: Merz 14**

Page 13: "Das Reich's" halftrack battalion was Regiment "Der Führer's" 3rd Battalion commanded by SS-Sturmbannführer Vincenz Kaiser. The other two battalions likely possessed some halftracks for special purposes but for the most part used trucks to transport their men and equipment. **KB: Merz 14**

Page 14: The car had been confiscated for use as an auxiliary vehicle by the division. The Germans used many civilian vehicles until they broke down or were destroyed. **KB: Merz 14**

Page 15: Russian planes were constantly in the air above the division's area along the length of the Belgorod-Prochorowka rail line but during the division's

move north Soviet air activity was light and there were few losses due to attacks by Russian fighter-bombers.
KB: Merz 14

Page 16 & 17: After the 167th Infantry Division's 315th and 331st Grenadier Regiments took over its positions, Regiment "Der Führer" mounted its halftracks and trucks and rolled northwards.
KB: Merz 14

Page 18: Almost half of the II. SS-Panzer Corps' tanks were Panzer IIIs, an obsolescent tank that was only marginally effective against the T-34 due only to improved armor and an upgraded main gun. The Panzer III was originally equipped with a 3.7cm gun but by the summer of 1943, most of these tanks were fitted with a high-velocity 5cm gun.
KB: Merz 14

Page 19: Track condition was critical in a combat situation. A broken or jammed track in the middle of tank battle could easily be fatal to both tank and crew.
KB: Merz 14

Page 20: Of the three SS divisions that took part in Operation Citadel, only "Leibstandarte" had more Panzer IVs than Panzer IIIs. The older model version remained the most numerous main battle tank of both "Das Reich" and "Totenkopf," which possessed 54 Panzer IIIs and only 30 Panzer IVs on July 11th.
KB: Merz 14

Page 21: "Leibstandarte" had 47 Panzer IVs and only five Panzer IIIs on the day before Prochorowka. In addition to these 52 tanks, the division had four operational Tigers and seven Befehlpanzers for a total of only 63 tanks.
KB: Merz 14

Page 22 & 23: The division maintained a company of T-34s until after the 1st Battalion of its Panzer regiment returned from training with the new Panther tanks in Germany. The battalion rejoined the division in August 1943.
KB: Merz 14

Page 24 & 25: These three Grenadiers seem to be very eager to share the contents of the mess kit. Instead of hot food, could it contain some liberated vodka? Note the grenade launcher spigot on the rifle slung over the man in the rear.
KB: Merz 14

Page 26: Most of the 167th Infantry Division's artillery was horse-drawn. With a few exceptions, only the Panzer and Panzergrenadier divisions of the Army and Waffen-SS were considered fully motorized. The vast majority of German divisions in Russia depended upon horse power to move their heavy weapons if rail travel could not be arranged.
KB: Büschel 146

Page 27: The divisions that were completely motorized possessed such a variety of different trucks, armored cars, tanks and other armored fighting vehicles that it was very difficult to stock the array of parts necessary to keep them all running.
KB: Büschel 146

Page 28: During the heavy fighting that raged back and forth over the area southwest of Prochorowka, many villages and towns were devastated, particularly along the flanks of II. SS-Panzer Korps. Much of the fighting took place directly in these villages leading to their destruction.
KB: Büschel 146

Page 29: Two SS men have requisitioned livestock and place a calf in the vehicle. When possible, soldiers supplemented their standard rations with whatever could be found while on the move.
KB: Büschel 146

Page 30: Even given their unique silhouette and seemingly distinctive size, the Tigers carried large flags to identify themselves to Luftwaffe dive-bombers and fighters. In spite of this attempt to show their identity, German planes attacked Michael Wittmann's Tiger during the fighting on July 7th. Only when Wittmann stood in his turret and waved his aircraft identification flag did the Stukas pull up from their attack.
KB: Büschel 146

Page 31: Many of the towns were fought over for days. Some changed hands repeatedly and thus were devastated by artillery fire, air attacks and destructive street fighting.
KB: Büschel 146

Page 32 & 33: On July 11th "Das Reich" reported that it shot down an IL-2 fighter bomber and a Lagg-3 fighter. Neither "Totenkopf" nor "Leibstandarte" reported downing any Soviet planes. "Leibstandarte" did report that its halftrack battalion had been attacked by German planes and had suffered significant casualties from the "friendly fire."
KB: Büschel 146

Page 34: The Soviet 12.7mm automatic cannon is very similar to the American .50 caliber machine gun. Both weapons are deadly when used by aircraft against unarmored vehicles and personnel. Even light armored vehicles such as halftracks were vulnerable to armor-piercing rounds.
KB: Büschel 146

Page 35: The men search the cockpit of the downed Russian fighter, searching for souvenirs or documents of importance. Although it apparently made a crash-landing, it does not appear structurally damaged and has not burned. The belts of 12.7cm ammunition are examined by one of the men, who perhaps wonders if the guns can be salvaged and mounted on a halftrack or truck.
KB: Büschel 146

Page 36: Someone has clearly staked his claim to the downed plane by writing a warning message on the tail in chalk.

"Nicht ausschlachten, wird repariert!!! denke an unseren Westen!"

Don´t cannibalize, will be repaired!!! Think of our west!
KB: Büschel 146

Page 37: In the woods east of "Das Reich's" positions loud tank motor noise had been heard clearly for much of July 10th-11th. This meant only one thing to the Grenadiers: sooner or later a massed Russian tank attack. With this prospect in mind, there are no smiles for the camera.
KB: Büschel 146

Page 38 & 39: The most common heavy artillery piece supplied to the artillery regiments of the Waffen-SS and Army was the sFH18 (heavy field howitzer, Model 18) which remained in service for the entire war, being modified numerous times.
KB: Büschel 150

Page 40: "Leibstandarte's" artillery was to shell Russian gun positions on each flank of the division's advance while Stukas provided close support to the attacking battalions. However, bad weather grounded the Luftwaffe and the division had to change its mission in support of the attack. This left the Russian guns on both

flanks free to fire upon the Grenadiers as they began their assault.
KB: Büschel 150

Page 41: In "Das Reich's" sector the divisional artillery fired barrages to distract the Russians while the exchange of positions with the 167th Infantry Division took place. In one instance however, the artillery fired in support of a counterattack made by SS-Sturmbannführer Hans Bissinger's battalion against a battalion strength Soviet reconnaissance in force.
KB: Büschel 150

Page 42 & 43: Perhaps the soldier was a driver or other member of the support units for the artillery. All members of a gun crew were involved in firing the gun, whether actually loading and firing the gun or carrying shells and preparing them for use.
KB: Büschel 150

Page 44: From July 11th, following the arrival of the 5th Guards Army north of the Psel River, "Totenkopf's" bridgehead was continuously attacked along its entire defensive front by Russian infantry and tanks. The artillery played a major role in turning back these assaults.
KB: Büschel 150

Page 46: Carrying shells could be an exhausting task, particularly in the stifling heat of the Ukrainian summer. It also required strength because each shell weighed slightly more than ninety-five pounds. "Totenkopf's" artillery regiment, after days of firing heavy concentrations of fire supporting the division's advance to the Psel River, was running short of ammunition by July 11th.
KB: Büschel 150

Page 47: Corps records note that the division's supply of artillery

shells was nearly depleted. On the morning of July 11th a cache of 1,000 10cm shells was located in the nearby town of Tomarowka alleviating somewhat the worry that the division would run out of ammunition for its guns at a critical time.
KB: Büschel 150

Page 48 & 49: This tank has had brackets welded to its sides in order to mount thin armored skirts over the wheels and tracks to furnish protection from shaped-charge shells. Note the large German cross painted on the side of the turret and the swastika on the turret hatch to aid in identification when viewed from the front.
KB: Büschel 150

Page 50 & 51: The picture clearly shows the rubber rimmed road wheels and "Christie" type suspension that was developed by an American engineer in the prewar years. When the American Army showed little interest in the design the inventor marketed it overseas.
KB: Büschel 150

Page 52: The man on the right is equipped with an array of items necessary for survival on the battlefield. Camouflaged helmet goggles for eye protection, Zeiss binoculars, camo smock and a pistol for close combat.
KB: Büschel 150

Page 53: Although the days were very hot and humid under the blazing sun, temperatures could drop drastically during the night. The standard wool overcoat came in handy during the night particularly during rain storms because wool insulates even when wet. In this case, the awake soldier wears a rubberized motorcyclist's coat, also helpful in providing warmth and comfort.
KB: Büschel 150

Page 54: As sergeants have told young soldiers ever since there have been sergeants and young infantrymen: a clean gun will save your life.
KB: Büschel 150

Page 55: The soldier on the right grins for the camera but most of the others seem to have more serious thoughts on their mind.
KB: Büschel 150

Page 56 & 57: On July 11th the three SS divisions captured 245 prisoners; 175 by "Das Reich" and listed 114 other Russian soldiers as deserters.
KB: Büschel 150

Page 58 & 59: Russian tank crews preferred Russian tanks over any of the British or American tanks supplied to the Soviet Union through the Lend-Lease program. Thousands of Grant, Sherman, Cromwell and other tanks were sent to the Soviets but all were inferior to the Russian T-34 and later heavy tanks such as the Stalin series.
KB: Büschel 150

Page 60: Armored cars and Horch heavy cars pause on the reverse slope of a hill before continuing over the crest. The reconnaissance battalions of the SS-Panzergrenadier divisions were made up of a mixture of heavy cars (right), armored cars (left) and halftracks. With their mobility and heavy weapons, they were potent fighting formations.
KB: Büschel 150

Page 61: An "Aufklarungs" battalion moves into battle! SS tanks grind forward towards the crest of a hill while halftracks carrying Grenadiers follow closely behind.
KB: Büschel 150

Page 62: A camouflaged Russian "Pakfront", one or more

batteries of 4.5cm or the more dangerous 7.6cm gun, was the tank crews worst enemy. Often firing at very close range from hidden gun positions, SS tankers feared this concealed enemy more than Russian tanks.
KB: Groenert 8

Page 63: During the battle of Kursk, Kaiser commanded "Das Reich's" 3rd Battalion of Regiment "Der Führer," the division's halftrack battalion. Kaiser was awarded both classes of Iron Cross, the German Cross in Gold, the Knight's Cross and later the Oak Leaves. He did not survive the war as he was listed as missing in action on April 20, 1945.
KB: Groenert 8

Page 64 & 65: Captured Russian soldiers or deserters were used by the tens of thousands in the SS and Army divisions to do all sorts of work. Many Russian soldiers gladly accepted food and shelter from their captors rather than imprisonment in a POW camp.
KB: Groenert 8

Page 66: There were few paved roads in southern Russia. In the summer they were either dusty, baked by the sun, or a morass of mud when the typical torrential summer thunderstorms drenched the area with huge amounts of rain.
KB: Groenert 8

Page 67: The Russian soldier faced a serious dilemma if he surrendered. If he went into captivity he would face starvation, exposure to the elements and overwork. However, to become a "Hiwi" (Russian volunteer in service to the Wehrmacht) was to sign his death warrant if recaptured by Soviet troops. This Russian seems to be clearly contemplating his choices.
KB: Groenert 8

Page 68: "Leibstandarte's" halftrack battalion (Peiper) was the only one of the three similarly equipped SS battalions to be engaged in combat on the day before the climatic battle of Prochorowka. Peiper's battalion was engaged in fighting against Russian tanks and infantry on the slopes of Hill 252.2. "Das Reich's" halftrack battalion was on the move to its new positions while "Totenkopf's" was waiting for the completion of bridges to be built across the Psel River capable of holding tanks.
KB: Groenert 8

Page 69: The large German cross on the side of the turret is easily visible on the turret of the tank on the right. Even with such identification German anti-tank gunners, who identify targets on silhouette, could easily mistake a "friendly" T-34 from one operated by a Russian crew.
KB: Groenert 8

Page 70: A Befehlpanzer, with the tank commander peering cautiously from the turret cupola, observes the course of the fighting as his tanks move into battle in the distance.
KB: Groenert 8

Page 71: Although Michael Wittmann is one of the best-known SS Tiger commanders, there were several other successful SS tank commanders who did not obtain celebrity status. On July 7th, "Leibstandarte" Tiger commander Franz Staudegger and his crew knocked out more than twenty T-34s of the Soviet 10th Tank Corps even though his Tiger could not maneuver well because of chassis damage.
KB: Groenert 8

Page 72: In heavy fighting a tank could use up its shells quickly. It was thus important that resupply was organized at every

opportunity in order to keep the tanks in action. The supply troops who delivered shells to the Panzers often had to bring up their cargo in the midst of a battle.
KB: Groenert 8

Page 73: One of "Das Reich's" most successful Tiger tank commanders was SS-Untersturmführer Hans Mennel, whose tank knocked out twenty-four Russian tanks in battle between July 7th-12th. Mennel was killed in action on July 14th.
KB: Groenert 8

Page 74: Many company and platoon commanders' vehicles were equipped with 20mm or 3.7cm guns mounted on the front of the vehicle. These were used to furnish close fire support to the attacking grenadiers.
KB: King 51

Page 75: On the morning of July 11 "Leibstandarte" attacked two fortified hills blocking the division's path to Prochorowka. One elevation, designated Hill 252.2 would be the seen of horrific fighting on July 12 during the legendary battle of Prochorowka.
KB: King 51

Page 76 & 77: Halftracks with automatic guns and a battery of self-propelled 15cm infantry guns of Peiper's battalion provide covering fire for the advance of the Grenadiers. SS-Untersturmführer Erhard Gührs commanded the 14th (heavy) Company that included halftracks equipped with 8cm mortars, 3.7cm anti-tank guns and a battery of six heavy 15cm infantry howitzers mounted on a tracked chassis ("Grille").
KB: King 51

Page 78: Obviously during a lull in the fighting (note the man standing on his vehicle in the distance) a motorcycle putters through the high grass of the

Ukrainian steppe, characteristically flat and dotted with small clumps of trees.
KB: King 51

Page 79: During pauses in combat, experienced combat soldiers seize any chance to rest, knowing that the fighting may continue into the night with little chance of sleep until the early hours of morning.
KB: King 51

Page 80: On July 12th, during vicious fighting against Soviet tanks which had overrun Peiper's battalion on the reverse slope of Hill 252.2, Wolff would win the Knight's Cross for his leadership and bravery after taking charge of a company whose commander had been killed moments before. He was formally awarded the decoration on August 7, 1943. Wolff was killed in action just prior to the end of the war.
KB: King 51

Page 81: The Churchill had reasonably heavy armor but the main gun was not adequate for combat in Russia. Its shell could penetrate the Panzer III's and IV's frontal armor only at close range and could not penetrate a Tiger at any distance.
KB: King 51

Page 82 & 83: Cromwells and Churchills were used by the Soviets primarily in heavy battalions attached to a tank brigade or corps. Russian troops preferred the more effective Soviet KV-1 that had better armor and a superior 7.6cm main gun. The KV's main drawback was that it was too heavy for many small bridges and slow.
KB: King 51

Page 84: While the man wearing the camoflage smock in the foreground cleans a number of mess kits, other men stand in line

in front of a village well which is located in the small log building.
KB: King 51

Page 85: A motorcycle crew has been sent with a "jerry can" to fill up with water. To the rear is a halftrack, its crew waiting for water also. To the right can be seen the rear of a Sturmgeschütz or Panzer III. The line of men in the background, some are without shirts while others carry buckets, seems to indicate that these soldiers don't expect "Ivan" to interrupt their water re-supply.
KB: King 51

Page 86 & 87: While his comrades stand in line, this crewman wearing a one-piece tanker's coverall operates the handle that pumps water for the rest of the men. In the heat of the Ukrainian summer, dehydration was a serious problem, particularly for the Panzergrenadiers exposed to the sun and the tank crewmen in the furnace of their tanks. Therefore clean, cool water was not only refreshing but a necessity of war.
KB: King 51

ARCHIVE SERIES

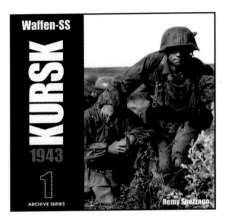

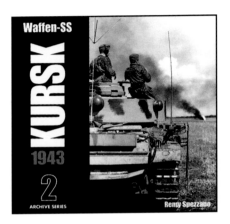

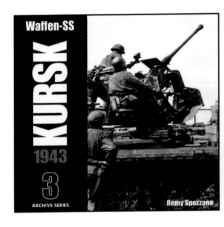

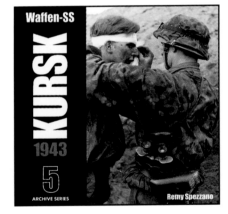